Learning Tree 1 2 3
Schools

By Natalie Swift
Illustrated by Tony Morris

CHERRYTREE BOOKS

Read this book and see if you can answer the questions at the end. Ask an adult or an older friend to tell you if your answers are right or to help you if you find the questions difficult. Often there is more than one answer to a question.

A Cherrytree Book

Designed and produced by
A S Publishing

First published 1993
by Cherrytree Press Ltd
a subsidiary of
The Chivers Company Ltd
Windsor Bridge Road
Bath, Avon BA2 3AX

Copyright © Cherrytree Press Ltd 1993

British Library Cataloguing in Publication Data
Swift, Natalie
  Schools.—(Learning Tree 123 Series)
  I. Title II. Series
  371

  ISBN 0-7451-5207-4

Printed and bound in Italy by L.E.G.O. s.p.a., Vicenza

All rights reserved. No part of this publication may be reproduced, stored in a retrieval system, or transmitted, in any form, or by any means without the prior permission in writing of the publisher, nor be otherwise circulated in any form of binding or cover other than that in which it is published and without a similar condition including this condition being imposed on the subsequent purchaser.

These children lived long ago.
What do you think they are learning about?

The first people lived in caves or in huts.
They could not read or write.

Children learned how to find plants to eat.
They learned how to kill wild animals.
They learned how to make a fire.

Teachers told the children stories.
They taught them about the sun and moon.
They told them about famous people and places far away.

In time people invented writing.
Lucky children learned to read and write.
They learned how to count too.

Only rich children had lessons.
These children lived in ancient Egypt.
Priests taught them about the gods.
They learned how to write in pictures.

In ancient Greece only boys went to school.
They went to the teacher's house for lessons.
They learned many subjects.
They had to be good at sports too.

In ancient Rome most children went to school.
They wrote on sheets of wax.
Next day they smoothed the wax and used it again.

Some children learned to be soldiers.
They all learned how to speak well.
They recited speeches to the class.

The first books were about religion.
They were written by hand.
Children had to study the holy books.
They learned them by heart.

Monks and nuns taught many children in the middle ages.
Boys learned Latin and how to copy the books.
Girls stayed at home and learned to sew.

The invention of printing made books cheap.
Many more children could learn to read.
Most children went to village schools.
One teacher taught them everything.

Children learned to read and write and do sums.
They learned history and geography.
They also learned how to behave.
If they were naughty they were punished.

Children did not have much fun at school.
Teachers were often very strict.
Classrooms were cold and gloomy.
Lessons were boring.

The pupils had to sit still on hard seats and learn facts by heart.
They were punished if they moved or spoke or made a mistake.

Today there is much more to learn.
But school is not so hard.
There are lots of books to read and write in.
There are calculators and computers.

Teachers try to make the lessons fun.
They like the children to enjoy learning.
Even very young children like going to school.
Some people stay at school until they are 18.

Schools have changed a lot since long ago.
But children still learn in the same way.
They listen to the stories that their teachers tell them.

More about schools

Ready for life
The first children learned how to collect food and make a fire. They learned skills that they would always need. Without food and heat, they would starve to death or freeze in winter. They also had to learn how to sew to make warm clothes.

Today children have to learn different skills. They need to know how to read books and newspapers. They need to be able to do sums and handle money. They also need to learn skills that will help them earn a living when they grow up. They may want to be teachers, scientists, cooks, computer experts or tennis players. Whatever job or career they choose, they need to learn special skills.

Learning for pleasure
Learning many different subjects helps people enjoy more of their life. Painting pictures and playing the piano are great fun. The more you practise them, the more enjoyment you get. If you are good at computer games, you have more fun playing them.

Education round the world
Many children in the world do not have books or go to proper schools. They sit outside in the open air and listen to the teacher. In some countries there is not enough money to pay for books or teachers, so children do not even learn to read and write. In some parts of the world, children listen to their lessons on the radio. They live too far out in the country to go to school.

Girls and boys
Once only boys went to school. Girls stayed at home. Their mothers taught them to cook and sew and do the washing. People thought that they did not need to know anything else.

The daughters of some rich families had private lessons. A tutor came to their house, or they had a teacher who lived at their home called a governess.

Today all boys and girls in this country go to school and have the chance to learn the same things.

1

1 Why do children go to school?

2 Where do you go to school?

3 Draw a picture of your school. Draw your teacher.

4 Why did the first children learn to make fires?

5 What do you wear to school?

6 What do these things help you to do?

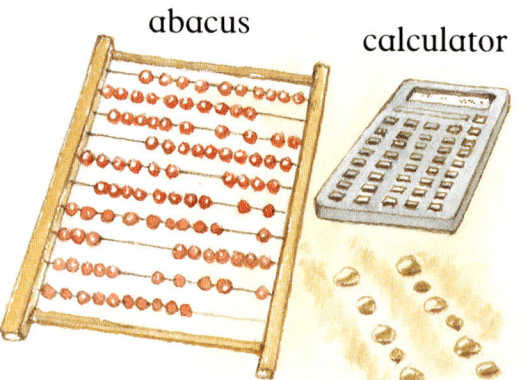

abacus

calculator

counting stones

2

7 What sort of clothes did the first children wear?

8 Why do you need to be able to count?

9 What did Egyptian writing look like?

10 Make up some picture writing of your own.

11 Did girls go to school in ancient Greece?

12 What did Greek boys need to be good at?

13 What did schoolchildren write on in ancient Rome?

14 Draw a Roman soldier.

15 What were the first books about?

3

16 Make a notebook for yourself. Put the answers to these questions in it. Think of other questions you want to ask about schools. Put those in your notebook. Draw pictures in your notebook.

17 Who taught children in the middle ages?

18 How were books made in the middle ages?

19 Write down what things you like about your school.

20 What is your classroom like?

21 Why was the invention of printing important?

22 What did children learn in the middle ages?

23 What is Latin?

24 Do people speak in Latin today?

25 What do Roman numerals look like?

26 See if you can find some Latin words or numbers on a building.

27 What was a village school like? Were there many teachers?

28 Do you think children in schools had much time to play?

29 What were their classrooms like?

30 What happened to naughty children?

31 Write a story about a day at school in the past.

Index

ancient Egypt 8
ancient Greece 9
ancient Rome 10
animals 5
behaviour 15
books 12, 13, 14, 18, 21
boys 9, 13, 21
calculators 18
careers 21
caves 4
class 11
classrooms 16
cooking 21
cooks 21
computer experts 21
computer games 21
computers 18
copying 13
counting 7
earning a living 21
education round the world 21
facts 17
famous people 6
famous places 6
fire 5, 21
food 21
geography 15
girls 13, 21
gods 8
governess 21
history 15
holy books 12
huts 4
jobs 21
Latin 13
learning by heart 12, 17
lessons 8, 9, 16, 19, 21
middle ages 13
mistakes 17
money 21
monks 13
moon 6
naughtiness 15
newspapers 21
nuns 13
piano playing 21
picture painting 21
picture writing 8
plants to eat 5
priests 8
printing 14
punishment 15, 17
pupils 17
radio 21
reading 4, 7, 14, 15, 18, 21
religion 12
rich children 8
rich families 21
scientists 21
sewing 13, 21
sitting still 17
skills 21
soldiers 11
speaking 11, 17
speeches 11
sports 9
stories 6, 20
strict 16
subjects 9, 21
sums 15, 21
sun 6
teachers 6, 9, 14, 16, 19, 20, 21
tennis players 21
tutor 21
village schools 14
washing 21
wax sheets 10
writing 4, 7, 12, 15, 18, 21